On the Beach

Written and illustrated by
Peter Haswell

Collins *Educational*
An imprint of HarperCollins*Publishers*

The Parish Church

Many centuries of history may be traced in Grantchester's church building. From about AD 1100 onwards, successive bouts of demolition and reconstruction reflect changes in religious practice. The chancel, with its light and elegant tracery, can be dated to c.1360 and is cared for by the church's patron, Corpus Christi College. On that college's coat of arms are images of both a pelican and lilies, their symbolism recalled in an old rhyme:

> Fit emblem in this bird I see
> Of Christ who shed his blood for me,
> And in the lilies undefiled
> The Mother of this Blessed Child.

They appear in the mosaic floor before the altar, together with the Tudor rose, which marks the village's long connection with King's College.

A great rood screen once separated the nave from the chancel, where, until the Reformation of the 1500s, Roman Catholic rites were celebrated. This carved screen, originally bearing a crucifix and kneeling figures of St Mary and St John (later replaced by the Royal coat of arms), survived until the late 18th century. The church's former medieval windows and carved and painted images of saints were all destroyed by Puritan zealots in the 1640s. By 1875 the church, with clear windows, looked exactly

▼ *The east end of the Church of St Andrew and St Mary stands above Mill Way.*

▲ This medieval 'green man' carving can be found high on the south wall, together with other ancient remnants.

as recorded in the scale model displayed near the gallery. In the following years a south aisle was added, the roof of the nave raised and Victorian stained glass installed.

Maintenance of the church fabric is continuous and entails frequent fundraising efforts. A list of the church's regular services can be seen on the board outside. Whilst Holy Communion and Family Services have been updated in style, the 1662 Book of Common Prayer is still used for Early Communion, Matins and Evensong. Visitors are made warmly welcome to all of our Sunday services.

▲ The church's south-west side seen from a corner of its churchyard.

▶ The 14th-century chancel is here seen with a display of flowers and fruit for Harvest Festival.

The Churchyard

These laid the world away; poured out the red
Sweet wine of youth; gave up the years to be
Of work and joy, and that unhoped serene,
That men call age; and those who would have been,
Their sons, they gave, their immortality.

War Sonnets
Rupert Brooke

The churchyard is a place of quietness and meditation. At its entrance stands the War Memorial, on which the names listed include that of the poet Rupert Brooke, whose poignant war sonnets appeared shortly before his own death in April 1915.

Walking around the churchyard, many small discoveries may be made by reading inscriptions on the graves. Grantchester, being so close to Cambridge, has long had associations with the university; many distinguished academics have been buried here among those rooted in the village for many generations. The tall 'pelican' column is a memorial to Fellows of Corpus Christi College.

▲ Looking downwards from the church tower (west side).

◄ The War Memorial, commemorating men of the village who died in the two World Wars.

4

The Manor Farm

▲ This tiny lodge stands at the entrance to Manor Farm.

▶ The ancient Manor Farm building.

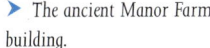

The Manor House is even older than it appears to be, with most of its original structure modified over the centuries. Bought by King's College in 1452, it was first used as a 'home farm', supplying the Fellows with provisions such as pigeons from the nearby 'Great Duffhouse', and vegetables and herbs from the 'Doctor's Garden' by the church wall. In time of plague, college Fellows took refuge here.

King's College, Lord of the Manor, gradually acquired the greater part of the village – farmland and buildings – and did much to conserve its character and contribute to its welfare. Once Grantchester's principal farm, Manor Farm is now absorbed in Trumpington Farms Ltd, some of its former outbuildings now converted into houses.

▶ Dove Cottage, whose high roof shows its earlier use as a pigeon-house.

The Orchard

For those who walk or punt to Grantchester, tea at The Orchard is a well-established tradition. It all began in 1897, when Mrs Stevenson was asked to provide tea for some young students at her lodging house there. This suggested the idea of starting a Tea Garden. As the success of the enterprise developed, she and her assistants were often kept busy from early morning until evening, first serving breakfast to couples who, after dancing all night at the end-of-term May Balls, came all the way up the river in punts, then serving the customary scones with honey from the Old Vicarage beehives for tea.

Today The Orchard offers morning coffee, luncheon and evening meals, besides the traditional afternoon teas. Dreamy and footsore couples still turn up for May Ball Breakfasts; in summer occasional outdoor theatrical events take place, too.

The orchard's fruit trees were first planted in 1868 by Mr Widnall of the Old Vicarage, who ate his 'first apple pie' that same year.

In the summer of 1909, Mrs Stevenson received a young graduate studying for a Fellowship at King's, Rupert Brooke, who took the bedroom nearest to the road. 'I'm in a small house,' he wrote, 'a sort of cottage, with a dear plump weather-beaten kindly old lady in control.' His many friends – styled as Neo-Pagans – often joined him for meals and exuberant discussion. Fading snapshots catch them at it: the Cornfords, Darwins, Oliviers, Raverats, Augustus John and Ka Cox; also members of the Bloomsbury Group – Virginia Woolf, Lytton Strachey, E.M. Forster, Maynard Keynes and Edward Thomas. Bertrand Russell and Ludwig Wittgenstein were later habitués.

Brooke, after two years, transferred next door to lodge at the Old Vicarage, where his idyllic Grantchester days continued: 'I bathe every morning and sometimes by moonlight, have all my meals (chiefly fruit) brought to me out of doors, and am as happy as the day's long.'

A collection of mementoes, together with items for sale, may be found in the small Rupert Brooke Museum in The Orchard House.

▲ *Mrs Stevenson, who first served teas in The Orchard, enjoys a cup with a friend.*

▼ *The Orchard in springtime.*

The Old Vicarage

▶ The Old Vicarage seen through its garden, with the 'Castle Ruin' folly on the left.

▼ The entrance to the Old Vicarage, at a bend in the Mill Way.

Beloved by Rupert Brooke, the Old Vicarage was not always appreciated by the clergy, for whom it had been built in about 1683 on the site of a far older rectory. Because it seemed 'small, in a low, bad situation', residence in the incumbent's other living was preferred. When, in 1850, the Rev. William Martin became Vicar, a new vicarage was provided, with ample space for servants and stabling for his horse and carriage. It was then that this house, now known as the Old Vicarage, was acquired by Samuel Page Widnall, son of a highly successful nurseryman and farmer.

S.P. Widnall, abandoning his late father's nursery business, devoted much of his energy to the creation of the garden that would so enchant Rupert Brooke. He built a Gothic 'folly', known as the 'Castle Ruin', to accommodate his many private pursuits. The upper part of this building became the 'Castle Theatre' for midwinter theatricals and a photographic studio where, from 1854 onwards, he took the likenesses of family and friends. Downstairs was the workshop where he practised various crafts – carpentry, metalwork, contriving mechanical devices and building his own boat. Most of his original constructions in the garden – glasshouse, Swiss Cottage, boathouse, fountain and bridges – have perished, but the ingenious sundial remains. He wrote several books, illustrating and printing them on a home-made printing press. Above all, we are indebted to him for his *History of Grantchester*, a remarkable work produced in 1875 to raise money for church improvements. In addition, his scale models of the church, Grantchester Mill, the Manor House and the Old Vicarage preserve for us an exact record of buildings now lost or altered.

Years after Widnall's death, Rupert Brooke moved into lodgings here. By now the house and garden were in romantic disarray and his delighted response appears in the poem *The Old Vicarage, Grantchester*, written in Berlin in a fit of homesickness. In his few years here he studied successfully, bathed in the river, pedalled off to neighbouring villages with political pamphlets for Beatrice and Sidney Webb, and gathered his friends, many later to be known as the Bloomsbury Group.

Travels abroad and war service took him away, but it was to the Old Vicarage that he dreamt of returning. On 23 April 1915 he died *en route* for Gallipoli, and after the Great War his mother, having lost all three of her sons, bought the house and entrusted it to Rupert's close friend, Dudley Ward.

The Ward family remained there until 1979, adding their own colourful inventions – mechanical singing birds, laboratory instruments, jewellery. The present owners, Jeffrey and Mary Archer, have enriched the garden with sculptures.

▲ *Rupert Brooke's own rooms in the Old Vicarage.*

◀ *Widnall's sundial, made in 1862.*

... there the chestnuts, summer through,
Beside the river make for you
A tunnel of green gloom and sleep
Deeply above; and green and deep
The stream mysterious glides beneath,
Green as a dream and deep as death.
   The Old Vicarage, Grantchester
      Rupert Brooke

People & Events

In Grantchester, some of us believe in keeping active! Barrel races on Boxing Day, apple-pressing in autumn, cricket and the Garden Fete in summer, cross-country running, a ceilidh to celebrate a Royal Wedding …

… and William Clamp still taking his daily walk at 105.

The Old Mill

For three centuries or more, a large watermill stood astride the bridge here. It was a busy place, turning corn brought by barges up the river or by horse-drawn wagons into sacks of flour. Ten or more men worked here, and by the 1900s its millstones were driven by oil-powered machinery in addition to its waterwheel. But in 1928 the mill caught fire and was totally destroyed in a blaze that could be seen for miles around. The present Old Mill was built as a replacement.

A long tradition was lost. The *Domesday Book* (AD 1086) records two mills in this parish, though neither at this spot. 'Our' Grantchester Mill, dating from a later period, was once owned by Merton College, Oxford, as part of that college's original endowment in the 13th century. Rent was paid partly in wheat, barley and eels trapped from the millstream.

▲ 'The Old Mill' replaces the great mill that once dominated this scene.

▼ An autumnal view across the millpool to Mill House.

▶ The philosopher
A.N. Whitehead and family
on the millpool below
Grantchester Mill, c.1905.

Among various interesting 20th-century residents of Mill House are Alfred North Whitehead, philosopher and mathematician, who worked there with Bertrand Russell on their *Principia Mathematica*; and David Robinson, who endowed Robinson College.

> ... Laughs the immortal river still
> Under the mill, under the mill?
> The Old Vicarage, Grantchester
> *Rupert Brooke*

The Meadows

For many people, the ideal approach to Grantchester is through the Meadows. A walk of just one mile takes one from the outskirts of the town to the village, with a refreshing change of scene on the way. Cattle are grazing, anglers crouch motionless under their huge umbrellas, swifts scream and swoop above, and along the river glide punts, swans and canoes. It is all very soothing.

▲ *Springtime on the Meadows.*

Once it was rather different, for most of our green meadows were divided into narrow, cultivated strips worked by several farmers before the Enclosures of 1800. The river, too, used to be a working thoroughfare along which occasional barges (with difficulty, surely) made their way up to the mill. The low-lying land was an attraction in those days for young men shooting ducks and snipe, to the annoyance of farmers whose crops they might damage. The more distant past is dim. An Anglo-Saxon settlement was excavated in the area near the back of The Red Lion, and both Roman and Bronze Age artefacts have been found in the village.

Walking, boating, kite-flying and picnicking grew in popularity about a century ago, when the trade of hiring out punts and skiffs began. This 'upper river' stretch

◄ *The gateway to the Meadows from near The Red Lion.*

▲ A punt makes its way along the Granta from Cambridge.

▼ The meadows are grazed by Red Poll bullocks. A thatched cottage and the low Almshouses are glimpsed beyond.

sometimes known, is taken by a variety of people: families with bounding dogs, undergraduates and elderly dons in deep conversation, and courting couples. An old village tradition, now ended, was the annual Grantchester Feast, when for two or three days each July there was 'all the fun of the fair' on the field near The Red Lion. In 1887 Queen Victoria's Golden Jubilee was celebrated on the Meadows with sports which included a Greasy Bowsprit across the river, dancing, and finally a boat decorated with fairy lights carrying revellers up to Byron's Pool. For Queen Elizabeth II's Silver Jubilee there were sports here too.

from Newnham to Grantchester can challenge the punter, especially in a head wind. Yet for the persevering, ignoring the diversion past the Old Vicarage to the millpool, their destination is Byron's Pool, where (being deeper in those days) the poet Lord Byron used to swim while an undergraduate at Trinity.

The 'Grantchester Grind', as the walk through the meadows was

In winter the meadows often flood, and in freezing weather there is tobogganing and skating. Just occasionally it has been possible to skate along the river as far as Cambridge and Ely.

Around the Village

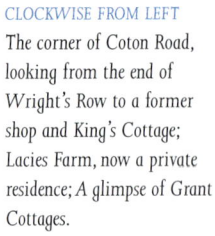

CLOCKWISE FROM LEFT
The corner of Coton Road, looking from the end of Wright's Row to a former shop and King's Cottage; Lacies Farm, now a private residence; A glimpse of Grant Cottages.

G rantchester gives the impression of being an 'unchanging' village, but that is not quite true. In earlier days its boundary extended further northward, including most of what is now Newnham, and by the early 1900s its population had grown to more than 1,000. In 1912 'New Grantchester' was separated from the present, old parish with a consequent drop in population. By the 1960s a need for more accommodation led to the building of an estate of family houses, as well as bungalows for the elderly with a Community Centre. The village now has about 600 residents.

Nowadays few of these people can make their living within its bounds. Gone are the self-sufficient years when the parish included several farmers, carpenters, brewers, a miller, a brickmaker, a tailor, a shoemaker, a blacksmith, a schoolmaster, a butcher and a baker, besides many other workers on the land, in the mill or in domestic service. That was the situation for generations, when many of its residents scarcely even ventured as far as Cambridge. But towards the end of the 19th century transport and education improved, both town and university grew prosperous, and movement became freer. Many now commute to Cambridge for their work, and some make a daily journey to London. A few have studios at home where they write, paint or engage in craftwork.

▼ *'Cobblers', once the home of a shoemaker.*

▲ Merton House.

▼ The White Cottage.

▼ Audley Cottage.

If you enter the village along the Newnham-to-Grantchester road, you first come to the Broadway, with its terrace of houses. These were built in 1878, partly in response to an influx of the extra labourers needed at that time for a curious industry: coprolite mining. It did not last for many years, though it did bring a burst of prosperity, since coprolites – 'phosphatic nodules' of fossilised dung from prehistoric animals – were found beneath this area and yielded valuable fertilizer for farming.

Past the Blue Ball pub is the former Baptist Chapel (1876), now attached to its neighbouring house – itself once two dwellings, the further of which has a dove loft. Next comes Audley Cottage, seeming to be just a pretty *cottage ornée* but with its own history as a small farm, a butcher's shop and then the village's post office. It actually has associations of great antiquity. Legal documents refer to farmland belonging to Ralph Audele in the 15th century, and the name occurs as far back as 1327; the field opposite the cottage is known as 'Audleys Close'.

A large timber barn stands end-on to the road. It is the last remnant of what was Merton Farm; and further along is Merton Farm Cottage, now all that survives of the once-extensive properties in Grantchester owned by Merton College, Oxford. After that, on the right, is Merton House, whose former residents include a Professor of Divinity and William Bateson, pioneer of the study of genetics. Opposite, a long, low building was originally a set of thatched Almshouses, where poor widows ended their days.

The view ahead shows the junction of Coton Road (from the right) with the High Street. Here is Wright's Row, now five cottages, though originally seven or eight. (A late Victorian census shows one couple living with nine children in one of these cramped dwellings!) Now, the Cottage Preservation Society cares for these and for 'Crossways', around the corner. They are typical of the cottages in this region once built at small cost by using 'lath and plaster' construction; and since these materials need constant renovation, most of those in Grantchester had fallen into decay and were demolished. Across the road, King's Cottage (for years divided into two dwellings) shows its age in its impressive chimney stack. Earlier in its history it may have served as the village's Guildhall.

Along the Coton Road is the entrance to the large housing estate where the greater number of the village's population live. It has family houses, a recreation ground, and bungalows for retired people. In designing the layout, names were chosen for its roads which recall village history – notable men (Widnall and Nutter) and the old field names (Stulpfield, Tabrum, Sladwell and Crome Ditch). Further on, on the opposite side, is Lacies Farm, which was active until 1992 but is now a private residence. The house front has an early 18th-century appearance, but the building actually has its origin in about 1620. Its large barn is dated 1798. On the way back towards the High Street, Scales Barn is a remnant of another of the village's once independent small farms.

Byron's Lodge, beside the Green Man, may or may not have an actual association with the poet. A Victorian occupant of The White Cottage, next door, traded as a butcher and also provided small carriages for hire. Beyond, Miller's Cottages were built for men working at Grantchester Mill.

The road takes a series of bends – thought to have arisen from the old layout of furlong strips of farm land – down to the bridge over the millstream by the Old Mill. It then winds between fields to Brasley Bridge crossing the river Granta, which marks the parish boundary with its neighbour, Trumpington.

A network of field paths and bridle tracks is now provided with signs to guide walkers from one village to another, and to the edge of Cambridge.

▲ This view is often people's first impression of Grantchester – Wright's Row at its junction with Coton Road.

▲ Some houses in Stulpfield Road. The name 'Nutters Close' recalls James Nutter, the last of Grantchester's millers.

◀ The end of the Bridle Way, where the track continues through fields to Barton.

The Old School & Village Hall

▶ *This small thatched building was the original Grantchester School. Now known as the Reading Room, it is attached to the Village Hall and is used for meetings and small gatherings.*

▼ *The gateway to the Victorian school, now a private house.*

The tiny National School built in 1830 (at a cost of £80) before long became crammed with some 100 children. Money was raised, and the grander 'Old School' across the road was built in 1867. Like its predecessor it carried a high bell tower, and since its one room still proved insufficient, another was added. One heroic teacher, Miss Charlotte Snelling, had sole charge for 38 years with only untrained girls for assistance. A good standard was maintained by her successors in spite of constant difficulties; but numbers gradually declined until, in the 1960s, the village's population increased with new housing. The school then developed a high reputation and a good-sized modern building was added. But then things went wrong; numbers dropped and in 1981 Grantchester School was closed, a great loss to the village.

The original little thatched schoolroom, meanwhile, became the village's Reading Room. In 1928 it was attached to a new Village Hall. Both are in constant use.

Farming

In recent years farming in Grantchester has altered in many ways. Where in Victorian times 35 men and 14 boys were employed by the two major farms, Lacies and Manor Farm (together 886 acres), now those and other areas of farmland are all managed by Trumpington Farms Ltd, with just two or three men.

This has been achieved by using the most advanced farm machinery and occasionally employing contract workers. The government-sponsored destruction of hedges in the 1970s created larger, prairie-like fields, more easily dealt with by machine. But more recently, the ecological ill-effects of reliance on artificial fertilizers and pesticides to increase yields have been recognised, and now some areas of wildlife habitat are left untouched. Skylarks, partridges and hares have returned. One low-lying field prone to flooding is now designated 'Trumpington Fen Wetlands', where a variety of birds – heron, snipe, little egret, lapwing – enjoy its rushes, grasses and wild flowers.

▲ A hare disturbed at harvest time.

◀ Sugar beet is harvested.

▼ The wheat harvest in progress.

Pubs

CLOCKWISE FROM RIGHT

The Blue Ball is Grantchester's oldest pub, although its present building dates from the 1880s; The Green Man has the oldest building, and is a good place to sit outside and watch the world go by; The Red Lion was once The Ax & Saw, but acquired its present name early in the 19th century. The present handsome building dates from 1936; The Rupert Brooke was given this name in the 1970s, having been known for many generations as The Rose & Crown.

FRONT COVER

Wright's Row, owned by the Cambs Cottage Improvement Society.

BACK COVER

This statue of Rupert Brooke stands in front of the Old Vicarage.

Acknowledgements

Text and photography by Christine Jennings.
Edited by Abbie Wood.
Designed by Jemma Cox.

© Grantchester Parochial Church Council
Publication in this form © Pitkin Publishing 2014.
No part of this publication may be reproduced, stored in a retrieval system or transmitted in any form or by any means without the permission of Pitkin Publishing and the copyright holders.

Printed in Great Britain.
ISBN 978-1-84165-563-5   1/14

Pitkin Publishing, The History Press, The Mill, Brimscombe Port, Stroud, Gloucestershire, GL5 2QG.

Enquiries and sales: 01453 883300
Email: sales@thehistorypress.co.uk
www.thehistorypress.co.uk

... Oh! Yet
Stands the Church clock at ten to three?
And is there honey still for tea?

The Old Vicarage, Grantchester
Rupert Brooke

ISBN: 978-1-84165-563-5